THE CREATIVE ART OF

Stencilling Designs

THE CREATIVE ART OF

Stencilling Designs

Caroline Green

Longmeadow Press

The Creative Art of Stencilling

This 1990 edition is published by
Longmeadow Press
201 High Ridge Road,
Stamford, CT 06904

ISBN 0-681-41006-X

© Salamander Books Ltd., 1990

0987654321

CREDITS

Editors: Jo Finnis and Judith Casey

Designer: Philip Gorton

Photographer: Di Lewis and Steve Tanner

Pattern artwork: Caroline Green

Typeset by: Barbican Print and Marketing Services Ltd.

Color origination by: Bantam Litho Ltd., England

Printed in Belgium by: Proost International Book Production

CONTENTS

INTRODUCTION

The aim of this book is to introduce beginners to the decorative art of stencilling and also to tempt experienced stencillers to use and enjoy a wealth of new designs. The designs range from very simple to quite complex ideas, and there are plenty of colourful step-by-step photographs and detailed instructions for you to follow for each project, together with patterns for all the stencil designs featured, ready to enlarge or trace directly from the book.

Stencilling is ideal for decorating a wide variety of household items including lamps, picture frames, fabrics and furniture. It is also an excellent method of decorating rooms, particularly those with uneven walls or odd-shapes, and for drawing attention to architectural features such as arches and exposed beams, especially in old houses. Modern houses take kindly to stencilling too, as this book shows, by giving some much needed character to otherwise boring and boxlike rooms.

One of the joys of stencilling is that it is a very personal art form. Two people using identical stencils will choose different colours, different ways of positioning the design and different techniques to produce something that is all their own. So, when you start a project, be sure to try out different colours and techniques first to get the best results from your stencil designs. If you are new to stencilling, begin with a small project, perhaps for a gift, and experiment until you gain enough confidence to attempt a whole room scheme.

T he materials for stencilling are many and varied. Pictured opposite is a selection of the paints, brushes and tools you will need. Some projects only require one brush, one pot of stencil paint, a knife and a small sheet of acetate, so the cost need not be daunting.

THE STENCIL

Virtually anything that masks out an area of background can be termed a stencil. You can use a pattern of masking tape, lace, paper doilies or even something with an interesting outline such as a leaf. The most usual thing to use is a cut-out stencil made from cardboard or acetate.

Stencil card is a brown, flexible, oiled cardboard that is very easy to cut, but opaque. This means you have to transfer the design directly on to it and that you cannot see through it to match up the design when stencilling. It is inexpensive, but becoming increasingly difficult to obtain as it has been superceded by modern plastic materials. It does not last very long when used with water-based paints but is excellent for sprayed designs.

Plastic film is usually referred to as acetate but its correct name is Mylar®. You can also buy large sheets or rolls of special film sold for use in drawing offices. This is very economical if you are going to do a lot of stencil cutting. You need a medium-thickness film so that it is strong enough to withstand a lot of use but not too thick to cut easily. You can also buy sheets of Mylar® ready printed with guidelines, especially for stencilling. All of these plastic films are transparent which means you can lay the film over a drawn design and cut straight through. You can also see through while stencilling, which is a great help when lining up a set of stencils.

EQUIPMENT

For cutting the stencil you will need a sharp craft knife with replaceable blades, or a scalpel available from art shops. A rubberized, self-healing cutting mat is the perfect base to cut on. It has a printed grid which is very helpful for drawing accurate guidelines and register marks, and it has a non-slip surface. Cutting mats are, however, rather expensive and a sheet of thick cardboard makes a good substitute.

Marking the film when making stencils is very important. You need guidelines and dotted lines for pattern matching that will stay on the film permanently. They need to be thin and accurate so a very fine, waterproof felt-tipped pen is ideal.

Low-tack masking tape is essential for stencilling. You can attach the stencils to the wall without damaging the surface, and mask areas of the stencil quickly and easily. You can also mend stencils which are accidentally torn or cut badly.

When it comes to painting your stencil, use specially made stencil brushes of the best quality; a selection of two or three sizes is available. After use, clean in the appropriate solvent for the paint, then wash in warm water and liquid detergent. Dry the bristles on an old towel and roll up in kitchen paper to hold the bristles in place until dry. Don't leave paint in the brushes to dry out or you will ruin them, and don't leave brushes soaking in water or you will loosen the bristles.

Real sea sponges can be used for making a sponged texture on walls prior to stencilling. Small pieces of the same (odd scraps or mis-shapen pieces are fine) should be used to create a mottled texture on larger stencils. Look after the sponges as you would brushes.

PAINTS AND CRAYONS FOR STENCILLING

There is a wide variety of paints suitable for stencilling, some made specifically for the job. Quick-drying stencil paints are ideal. They are water-based for easy cleaning, quick drying for speedy working and they come in a good range of colours. They are very economical and you can use them sparingly to produce a subtle cloudy effect or build up layers, making it possible to stencil a pale colour over a dark background. They are also intermixable so you can make virtually any colour you need.

Stencil crayons are large oil-based crayons that produce a soft effect when applied with a stencil brush. They are very easy for a beginner to use as there is no danger of runny paint leaking under a stencil. The colours blend beautifully and can be quite subtle or bold.

There are several sorts of fabric paints available, all water-based. They are either of a jelly consistency or fairly liquid, and are easy to use with a stencil brush or sponge. Lustre paints can be used on their own for a pale pearly effect or with metallic 'bronzing' powders for a shiny metal finish such as gold, silver or copper. Most fabric paints need fixing with a hot iron to make them washable.

Ceramic paints can, with care, be used to decorate tiles, ornamental china, vases and lamp bases but, because they are not fired, they do not stand up to hard wear and lots of washing, so bear this in mind.

Other suitable paints include ordinary household emulsion paints. They can be used on large, simple designs and can be applied with a sponge. Cellulose car spray paints can be used on walls, floors, metal surfaces, plastics and fabrics, and come in a surprising array of plain and metallic colours. They are very durable and you can blend the colours as you are stencilling, but you must mask around the stencil carefully to avoid overspray. Household spray paints are similar but, unlike car sprays, they come in pastel shades such as pink and peach. Artists' acrylic paints are good for flexible surfaces such as roller blinds and shower curtains. They are sold in tubes in a wide range of colours.

Once you have designed or selected your stencil image, one of the first things you may need to do is enlarge (or reduce) the design. This is easily done by a method known as squaring up. First draw a grid of squares over the design – many of the designs in this book are printed on a grid for this purpose. Now draw another grid of the same number of squares on to plain paper, or use ready-made graph paper. Make the squares either larger or smaller than the first grid, depending on the size you want the finished design to be. For instance, if you want it twice the size, make each square twice as large as the first ones. Then copy the design, one square at a time, noticing where each design-line crosses the grid lines, thus keeping the shapes in proportion. Draw the main outlines first and fill in the details afterwards.

Once complete, you can trace your design on to acetate using a fine waterproof felt-tipped pen. Alternatively, you can just tape the design under the film. When using stencil card, you will have to transfer the design with carbon paper, re-drawing over the shapes afterwards.

On complex multicoloured designs you will need to make a separate stencil for each colour. Trace around all the areas in the same colour and then just trace parts of the rest of the design with a dotted line. On repeating border stencils, draw a little of the adjoining design either side of the cut out areas to help you line up the next piece of stencilling. Always leave a good margin of uncut material around your stencil to allow for register marks and guide lines, and to prevent the colour getting accidentally spread on to the work surface at the edges.

To cut the stencil, use a sharp craft knife or scalpel and work on a cutting mat or thick cardboard. Hold the knife so that you are just cutting with the tip of the blade and turn the stencil so that you are always cutting towards you. When cutting around curves, move the acetate around the blade, rather than the knife itself. Start cutting at the centre of the design and remove the small areas first, so as not to weaken the stencil too much.

Brush stencilling on hard surfaces is the traditional method of stencilling, producing the familiar speckled texture. Use a good quality, flat, or slightly domed, stencil brush. Pour a little paint into an old saucer and dip just the tips of the bristles into it. Dab off some of the excess paint on to a piece of kitchen paper and you are ready to stencil. Tape the design in place and, holding the brush upright, dab on the paint with a gentle 'bouncing' movement. Make sure the edge of the

Choose a design motif from a piece of fabric, wallpaper, giftwrap, a book or a magazine, then carefully trace the shape on to tracing paper.

Now convert the motif into a stencil by redrawing it with 'bridges', so that whole areas of the design are enclosed within a continuous line.

stencil area is coloured to maintain the outline of each shape, but you can leave the centre of each area very pale. Don't put on a thick layer of paint but build up the colours in certain areas to look like shadows, giving your design a three-dimensional quality. Check progress by lifting the stencil occasionally and you'll find it is surprising how little paint you need to hold the design.

Brush stencilling on fabric is very similar to working on hard surfaces but you must make sure your fabric is washed, ironed and taped or pinned out flat on an absorbent paper-covered work surface. Natural fabrics are best. Tape the stencil very lightly to the fabric and work with the minimum amount of paint on the stencil brush to avoid it spreading under the stencil. When using the metallic finishes, dip the brush into the lustre paint and wipe off the excess. Tip a tiny amount of the metallic powder on to a piece of velvet and spread it out evenly over the fibres. Dab the brush into this, shake off any excess and then stencil. Don't mix the powder directly with the lustre to form a paste.

Oil-based stencil crayons also need brushes to stencil the colour. First break the clear seal on the tip of the crayon by rubbing it on to rough paper. Then scribble some of the colour on to an uncut corner of the stencil and rub the stencil brush into this to collect the colour. Rest the bristles lightly on the stencil and use a circular movement to spread the colour from the edges of the design into the centre. You can blend the colour very easily before the crayon sets but use a clean brush for each colour to avoid a muddy finish. Leave the design to set for a few hours to avoid any smudging.

Sponge stencilling is an ideal method of stencilling on emulsion painted walls when using a large open design. The sponge is simple to use, especially for a beginner, and the instant mottled texture is very easy to control. Always dip the sponge in water and squeeze out all the moisture before you start, to make the sponge soft and pliable. Pour a little paint into a saucer and dip the sponge into it. Dab off the excess on to spare paper and then stencil with a very light dabbing motion.

It is very important to clean the surface of your stencils from time to time, otherwise the build up of paint will eventually close up small holes in the design and make the edges ragged. Use the appropriate solvent, wiping the paint off on to waste paper. When you want to reverse the stencil, you must clean the surface thoroughly to avoid transferring paint on to the design surface in the wrong place.

If you wish to enlarge a design, first draw a grid of squares over it. Now, using a set-square, draw an enlarged grid on a piece of plain white paper.

Copy the design on to the new grid, square by square, paying particular attention to where the design lines enter and leave the squares.

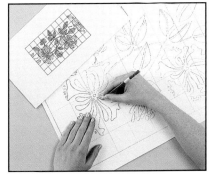

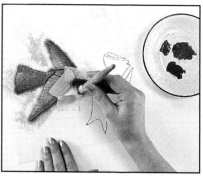

Choice of colour plays an important part in stencilling – here, a change of colour scheme has converted two bluebirds into Christmas robins!

To change the colour scheme of an existing stencil, don't bother making a new one – simply mask off the unwanted areas of the old stencil.

If you are a beginner, you will probably want to follow several of the designs featured in this book exactly, perhaps just changing the colours to suit your decor. But when you gain confidence, you will doubtless look around for other designs and ideas to employ. Look everywhere for design inspiration – flowers, plants, architecture, fabrics, china, tapestry, postcards, magazine cuttings and catalogues – the list is endless. It is for you to select and adapt.

When decorating a house, notice surrounding features that can be adapted and used as a stencil design. Look at decorative railings, cornicework, balustrades, bannisters, a special tree in the garden or clematis climbing up the wall; any of these can be turned into a stencil by drawing and stylizing the shapes. Alternatively, if drawing seems too difficult, find existing wallpaper, fabrics, tile designs or anything that takes your fancy.

For instance, if you have a favourite curtain fabric that you would like to use as a starting point for a stencilled roller blind, you will first need to trace off parts of the design, choosing a single motif such as a sprig of flowers, or a decorative bird. Similarly, you may wish to pick out one part of the design to use as a repeating border to stencil above a dado rail or around a door frame. Trace the design carefully and enlarge or reduce the size, as necessary, depending on the project. Always keep your initial designs and tracings as they may come in useful for future projects in different colours or applications.

To translate your design into something that can be cut out and stencilled, you need to simplify and adapt the shapes so that you can add 'bridges' to the design. Bridges are small spaces between parts of

How you position your stencils relative to each other can greatly affect the finished look of your design. For example, this corner design (taken from page 87) can

either be positioned to form a rectangle or square (as above) or positioned back to back (below) to create a very pretty border design.

the design that give the characteristic look of stencilling and add strength to the material out of which you are cutting the design. A long curving stem, for instance, should have several bridges across it to stop the material moving as you stencil – any movement would allow paint to creep underneath.

VARIATIONS

When you have tried some of the stencils by the methods described in this book, try out other variations for yourself. You will find these experiments are a worthwhile way of making full use of the stencils you have cut.

Colour makes a great deal of difference to the feel of the design as you can see here. The bird and bow design opposite was originally designed for the Lloyd Loom chair (see page 44) and was sprayed in pale peach and white. However, it looks delightful as a Christmas motif if you mask off the birds' breasts so that you can change them into robins. Stencil the main part of the body in light brown and the breast in red. The bow looks rich and satiny stencilled in green, with subtle darker shaded areas making it look almost real. Use this motif at any size to decorate special table linen for a Christmas party, a border around the room or even as a central design on a chimney breast.

You can also alter the relative positions of your stencils. Look at the corner design for the photo frame on page 20. It's interesting how different this can look placed back to back to make a border design or close together in pairs to make an oblong pattern. Try out some of these ideas on large sheets of paper to get the most from your designs.

S tencil your own wooden presentation boxes to add a little extra to a small gift. Choose single motifs and use either quick-drying stencil paints or stencil crayons. Mask off a small motif from a larger stencil and tape the acetate in position to complement the box shape. Stencil the box top and sides, mixing designs to create an attractive arrangement.

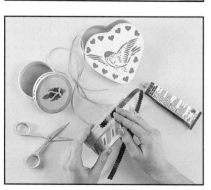

Make a coloured border on the lid by cutting a piece of cardboard slightly smaller than the box top, placing it centrally and stencilling around the edge. Finish off the box by gluing on lengths of satin ribbon, bows or self-adhesive parcel ribbon. You could also line the box with coloured tissue paper.

Making your own wrapping paper is great fun for a beginner at stencilling. Choose small, all-over motifs (see pages 47 and 92) and stencil with one or two different coloured stencil crayons. Use plain art paper and work across it, lining up the motifs as shown. Rub the crayon on the corner of the acetate and then collect the colour on to a stencil brush for stencilling.

Gold spray on dark paper makes a rich, dramatic gift wrap ideal for a man's Christmas present. Use the same stencil design but tape lining paper around the edge to act as a mask. Spray lightly through each motif, wait a few moments for it to dry, then move on to the next area. Matching gift tags can easily be made by cutting out one motif and gluing it on to folded cardboard.

Stencil this attractive iris design on to thick watercolour paper for a linen texture and use wax stencil crayons for subtle colour shading. Size up the design on page 86 and cut three stencils for mauve, yellow and green areas. Tape the green stencil in place and blend together two green crayons. Rub the crayons on to the acetate and then collect the colour on to the brush.

Remove the green stencil and tape the mauve one in position, lining up the vertical and horizontal marks. Blend mauve, blue and turquoise for the flowers, shading the lower petals in mauve and the upper ones in blues, and getting deeper towards the centre of each flower. Lastly, use the yellow stencil. Work the brush in a light circular motion to shade the colours throughout.

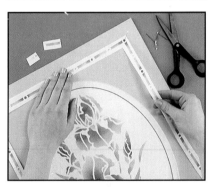

Have an oval mount cut to fit around your stencil. Cut out the border stencil from the design on page 87 and try it out on scrap paper in various colours. Cut these trial pieces into strips and lay them around your mount. Hold them in place with masking tape and then insert a pin centrally at each corner when you are happy with the position.

Carefully remove the strips and, very lightly, mark guide lines for stencilling the border using a pencil and set-square. Check the lines are exactly the right distance from the oval shape and parallel to the outer edge. The stencils at the top and sides should be equidistant from the oval and the lower stencil slightly further away to look visually correct.

Finally, stencil the border in a single colour using stencil crayons as before. Build up the colour where the strips meet the round spots in the design to add interest. Assemble the stencil with the mount and a piece of glass in a simple frame coloured to complement your flowers and decorations.

Terracotta flower pots are an ideal medium for stencilling, especially as a beginner's project. Match the designs to your room stencils, or make an attractive mixed collection to arrange in the garden, conservatory or on a patio. Choose small areas from your stencil patterns and repeat these around the pots, or simply sponge paint the pot, masking out areas to leave the terracotta showing through. Create your own designs with simple paper shapes attached with adhesive putty (e.g. Blu-Tack) and strips of masking tape in zig-zag designs. The best paint to use is an oil-based eggshell which will not be damaged when you water your plants. It is also hard wearing, ideal for outside use.

To decorate a pot to co-ordinate with the Honeysuckle Bathroom (pages 68–75), trace off small areas of the large honeysuckle pattern on page 71. Choose single leaves, small flower clusters and groups of two or three leaves. Cut out these stencils in small off-cuts of acetate so that you can position them easily on the curved sides of the flower pot.

Sponge the pot lightly all over in cream eggshell paint. When dry, repeat sponging in pale apricot for a soft mottled base coat. Position stencils in a random design and use masking tape to hold in place. Stencil designs with stencil paints and a large brush, shading from light to dark green on leaves and yellow to pink on flowers. Spray with clear varnish when dry.

For a simple striped design, press strips of wide masking tape vertically down the lower part of the pot and one strip around rim. Sponge exposed areas of pot with eggshell paint, dabbing off excess paint on to a piece of spare cardboard. Start with a coat of pale green then darker green on top. Carefully remove the tape and add a row of tiny stencilled hearts (page 87).

Make this pretty Victorian-style frame for a treasured photo. Using the design on page 87, draw up the shape of your photo frame on to thick cardboard and cut it out. Cut out a larger piece of wrapping paper and lightly draw the cardboard shape centrally. Cut out one stencil for each colour and lay them in place on the paper. Mark the horizontal and vertical guidelines.

Using pink and green stencil crayons, stencil two opposite corners with flowers and leaves. Rub the crayons on to acetate and then load the brush with the colour for stencilling. Clean the stencils with a rag dipped in white spirit. Then turn the stencils over and use them for the other two corners. Glue the cardboard shape in place on to the back of the stencilling.

Fold over the edges of the paper to the back of the card and glue in place. Cut the central area of paper and snip in towards the oval window. Glue these flaps to the back of the card to neaten. Tape the photo in place and cover another piece of cardboard in the same paper to make a backing piece. Make a narrow stand, cover in paper and glue to the back to complete.

Hang a wall vase on a plain white wall and stencil a bunch of flowers that will last all year. Draw out the design to size from page 89 and cut four stencils, one for each colour. Mark a pencil line where the top edge of the vase will be and tape the first stencil in position. Rub the stencil crayon on to the acetate and collect the colour on to a stencil brush. Stencil with a circular motion.

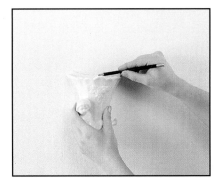

Tape the other stencils on, one by one, lining up the outlines to register the shapes accurately. Shade the colours slightly darker where the leaves twist and blend the colours into each other for a subtle effect.

Lift the stencil occasionally to check the result, going back to deepen the colour if necessary. Leave the stencil colour to set hard for about a day before positioning the vase to avoid smudging.

A plain pine mirror frame has been stencilled to echo the wall border. The design has been taken directly from the border by tracing off three or four motifs and simplifying the shapes slightly to make them easier to cut out as stencils. If necessary you can reduce or enlarge the size of the design to fit your mirror frame using the squaring up method.

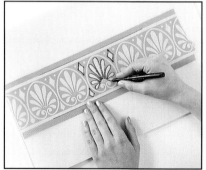

Try out your design on paper and work out the correct way to angle the motifs to fit the corners. Make two stencils – one for each colour. First trace off the design with a waterproof felt-tipped pen on to an acetate sheet. Then cut out the relevant pieces with a sharp craft knife on a cutting mat. Mark lines top and bottom on both stencils to line them up correctly.

When you have cut the stencils, lay them on to your paper pattern and mark a dotted pen line at a 45° angle at the end of the main motifs to align the corner motif. This will also line up with the mitred corner of the frame so that the spacing of the border is correct when you are positioning the main stencil. Now protect your mirror with a sheet of paper taped in place.

Start with the main motif and stencil along one side. Use quick-drying stencil paints blended to the correct colour and a small stencil brush. At the corner, twist the stencil and position one main motif across the corner. Mark the inner edge of the mirror on the stencil to align the other corners. Apply the second colour next, then finish with a coat of clear varnish.

Patterned china was the influence for the strawberry stencil used to decorate a new pine tray. Either use this design and purchase china to go with it or follow these instructions for designing your own stencil to match existing china. Start by taping small scraps of tracing paper to the china and tracing off single leaves, flowers and fruit.

Using the tracings, arrange the various elements of the design into a pretty group and draw the outline. Referring to page 87, turn this drawing into a stencil by creating 'bridges' in the design. Colour it to get the full effect and then make a separate stencil for each colour. Draw all the outlines on each stencil with a fine pen to line them up accurately. Cut out the stencils.

Sand the tray smooth before stencilling. Use the green stencil first, turning it as you work around the tray so that the design interlocks at the corners. Use quick-drying stencil paints and a small stencil brush for each colour. Dip the brush into the paint and wipe off the excess. Then stencil with a firm dabbing stroke to create a speckled texture.

Work one corner at a time, using both green stencils, followed by red then white. Make yellow the last colour as it overlays the other stencils. Leave for a few moments between colours to avoid smudging the paint. You can use small parts of the design to decorate narrow areas around the handle and on the tray sides. When the stencilling is complete, apply clear varnish all over the tray.

U se a short length of expensive lace as a ready-made stencil to decorate a delicate design on to any amount of bedlinen – sheets, pillowslips or duvet covers. Starting at one end of the wide hem on a sheet, pin on the lace so that the decorative lace edge runs along the edge of the fabric. Tape the two short ends and the straight edge of lace to mask from the spray.

Remove the pins. Lay the sheet on waste paper and mask all around with more paper to soak up overspray. In a small jar, mix black fabric paint (e.g. Color-Fun) with water to give a thin, very liquid consistency. Using a mouth-spray diffuser, blow the dye carefully over the lace. Aim for a light grey, spotty texture that will spread into the fabric. Leave to dry.

Move the lace along the edge of the sheet and mask and spray to complete the border. Remove all masking and leave to dry for 24 hours. Then use a hot iron to fix the dye. Pin and stitch lengths of grey and peach satin ribbon parallel to the lace edging to decorate further. Alternatively, choose coloured ribbon to match your decor.

Position, mask and spray the lace, in the same way, around the edge of the pillowslips. When you reach a corner, mask across the lace with tape at a 45° angle to mitre it. Match the lace pattern with the previous side where it meets at the corner. Finally, decorate with ribbons to match the sheets.

Create a stylish tile effect for a shower or bathroom with this intricate stencil design. Using the pattern on page 90, draw and cut out an acetate stencil for each colour. Carefully mark horizontal and vertical lines for the tile edges around the design to help line it up accurately on the wall. Use a waterproof felt-tipped pen.

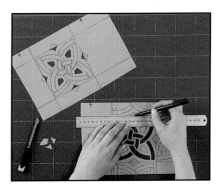

You will need to pencil mark the tile outlines on the wall before you start stencilling. To speed up this process, you can mark and cut out a piece of cardboard to use as a template, as shown. Join up all the marks with a long ruler to create an accurate grid.

Starting at the top, stencil the first colour along horizontally. Use quick-drying stencil paint in turquoise. Dab on with a nearly dry brush for a soft, even texture. Make sure the design is lined up exactly each time and wait a few moments for the paint to dry before moving on. Complete this colour all over the area. Leave to dry.

Use the second stencil for the green, working as before until complete. When this is dry, use a thick, green, waterproof felt-tipped pen and draw in the lines between the tiles to look like grouting. To complete, mask two lines with tape above the tiles to make a border. Stencil in blue and green. Cover the area with clear polyurethane varnish to protect the stencilling from water.

Stencil a plain white shower curtain with a complementary border design. Use only the turquoise stencil sheet and work one row of motifs about 10cm (4in) from the edge of the curtain. Use artist's acrylic paint, mixing the colours to match the tiles, and a stencil brush. This paint is water-resistant and will flex with the fabric. Mask a narrow border line and stencil in green.

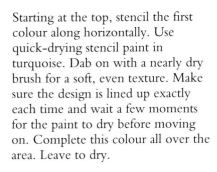

This lovely light sitting-room looked rather bare with plain walls, despite the number of pictures decorating it. To give it an outdoor feel, a trellis design has been stencilled in panels just below the coving. These panels give a definite area within which to hang the pictures, making the most of the pictures visually.

The wisteria design is stencilled in a random fashion over the trellis so that you can 'grow' as many flowers as you like. On page 89 there's one stencil design for the large blossom and one for the smaller spray with accompanying leaves and buds. By using all or part of these and

turning the stencils over, you can create an infinite variety of groups of flowers. Very natural colours are used here to mimic the real garden shades but you could just as well stencil the leaves in grey and the blooms in shades of pink and peach to match existing furniture and drapes. Alternatively, you could paint the flowers pale yellow suggesting a laburnum tree rather than wisteria.

The accessories such as the curtains, lamp and cushions have all been stencilled to complement the trellis design and make the room feel part of one whole theme, using colours and styles to bring it all together .

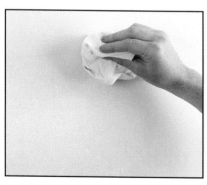

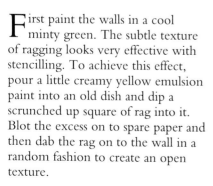

First paint the walls in a cool minty green. The subtle texture of ragging looks very effective with stencilling. To achieve this effect, pour a little creamy yellow emulsion paint into an old dish and dip a scrunched up square of rag into it. Blot the excess on to spare paper and then dab the rag on to the wall in a random fashion to create an open texture.

Measure a little way down from the coving or ceiling and cut a cardboard template to mark this distance around the room as shown. This will help you align the top of the stencil. Enlarge the stencil designs on pages 89, 94 and 95 using the squaring up method. Next cut the stencils: two end trellis pieces and one joining piece; one large and one small wisteria stencil; and one leaf stencil.

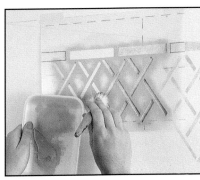

Start by taping the two end trellis stencils on to the wall and then mark where the joining piece will go, adjusting the ends to fit the design exactly. Mark lightly in pencil. Begin stencilling at one end using quick-drying stencil paints. Stencil very lightly in pale grey and accentuate the colour where the struts go under each other to look like a shadow and give a 3-D effect.

Position the wisteria and leaf stencils randomly to make large and small bunches. Start at a corner and work towards the trellis centre, waiting for the paint to dry before you overlap the next stencil. Mix the colours so that you get a varied range from blue to mauve in the flowers and several shades of green leaves. Clean the stencil with a damp cloth to use the reverse side.

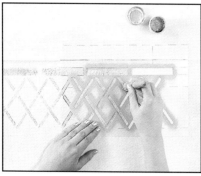

T he pelmet is made of stiffened calico to match the curtain fabric. You need a piece of calico about 56cm (22in) wide, and 60cm (24in) longer than your window. Fold the fabric in half along the length and stencil the joining trellis motif 2cm (¾in) down from the fold. Use grey fabric paint, dabbing it on lightly with a stencil brush for a speckled texture.

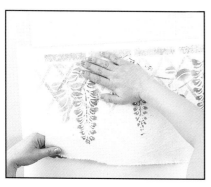

Stencil the flowers and leaves, keeping below the fold line. Leave to dry and then iron to fix the fabric paint. Cut a piece of self-adhesive pelmet stiffening about 5cm (2in) shorter than the stencilled fabric. Peel off the backing paper and press the fabric on to the stiffening, making the top edge of the stiffening run along the fold. Smooth out any air bubbles.

Peel the backing paper off the reverse side and press the fabric on to the back. Turn in the ends to neaten. Draw a line just below the trellis and then cut along this and around the flowers. Fix a strip of Velcro along the reverse side of the top edge and attach the matching half of the Velcro to a pelmet rail positioned so that the trellis on the pelmet lines up with the wall border. Press in place.

U se the flower and leaf stencils to decorate a plain coolie lampshade to go with your wisteria trellis room. Start with a spray of leaves and then add the flower spray. Work around the shade to make a balanced pattern. Use fabric paints and stencil very lightly so that the light will shine through and bring out the colours rather than making a dark silhouette.

Decorate the pottery lamp base too using the curtain border motif. Tape the stencil carefully around the lamp so that it does not slip. Stencil lightly with peach coloured ceramic paint. Leave to dry, then shade with a light coat of mauve paint. Adjust the border stencil so that it meets up around the lamp without leaving a gap. Leave to dry for 24 hours, then varnish to complete.

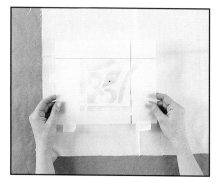

These cream silk cushions are stencilled in metallic fabric paints and quilted to make sumptuous accessories. Draw up and cut out the quarter design stencils from page 90. Mark the horizontal and vertical lines on the stencil and match these up with central pressed folds on a 48cm (19in) square of cream Honan silk. Tape the silk in place on a worktop protected with paper.

Tape the stencil in position and dip the brush into pearl, gold or silver lustre. Wipe off the excess and dip into gold powder. Shake off any excess and stencil with a light dabbing stroke. Move the stencil around the silk, lining up the marks with the creases in the silk each time to complete the pattern. Leave the paint to dry for about 24 hours, then set with a hot iron.

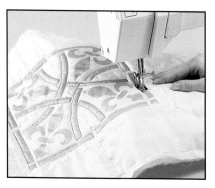

Cut a piece of polyester wadding the same size as the silk. Tack the layers together with several rows of stitching to hold securely in place. Using a sewing machine, stitch around some or all of the stencilled motifs to quilt them. Pull all the threads to the back, tie and cut off. Cut two backing pieces of silk 25cm x 48cm (10in x 19in). Turn under one long edge on each piece.

With right sides together and raw edges matching, pin and stitch the two backing pieces to the cushion front. Trim the wadding from the 1.5cm (⁵/₈in) seam allowance and turn the cover right side out. Press lightly. Stitch parallel rows around the cover through all the layers to make a 6cm (2¹/₂in) wide border. Insert a 30cm (12in) cushion pad and hand stitch the opening.

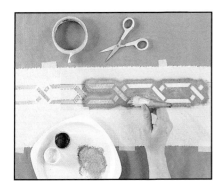

Trace and cut out the border stencil on page 91 to make a decorative padded edging for plain calico curtains. Cut a piece of calico 25cm (10in) wide and the length of each curtain. Tape the fabric flat on the work surface and lightly stencil in mauve to match the wisteria stencil. Place the stencil to print 4.5cm (1¾in) from one raw edge of the fabric.

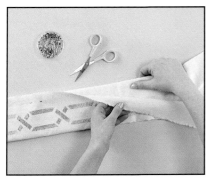

Leave the stencilled fabric to dry and then fix the paint with a hot iron. Fold the fabric in half lengthwise and lay a double thickness of curtain interlining or bump between the layers of calico. This should be the same width as the folded calico. Pin the top layer and the interlining together along the raw edge to hold in place.

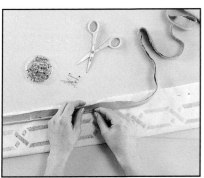

Make up some piping using narrow cord and a bias strip of toning chintz or repp. Pin and stitch this to the top layer of calico and the interlining. Pin this, right sides together, along the leading edge of your curtain and stitch close to the piping cord. Fold the free edge of the border to the reverse side of the curtain, turn in the raw edge and slipstitch to finish.

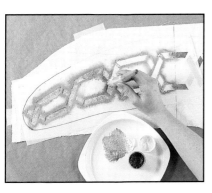

Enlarge and cut out the tie-back stencil, marking the outline of the shape on the acetate. Mark a line halfway across the calico and stencil as for the curtain border, using fabric paints. Leave to dry and fix with a hot iron. Cut out a piece of pelmet stiffening to the tie-back shape, remove the backing and press on to the back of the stencilled calico.

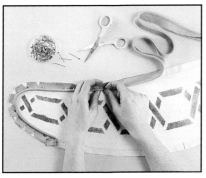

Trim the excess calico leaving 2cm (¾in) all around. Pin on covered piping cord, matching raw edges and clipping the curves. Stitch around the edge, close to the cord. Remove the other backing sheet and fold the seam allowance to the back. Cut another calico tie-back, press under the raw edge and slipstitch to back of the stencilled tie-back. Stitch a small ring to each end.

──BLUEBIRD BEDROOM──

T ransform an old attic into a dream bedroom, perfect for a little girl of any age. The detailed bluebirds are reminiscent of early Japanese designs and look charming with or without bows. This is a most adaptable design which is especially useful in a room of this style with lots of varying ceiling levels and roof angles to take into consideration. Notice the angled design leading up to the bedhead (which, incidentally, used to be a chimney breast). The birds forming this border are adapted from the right-hand bird on the original stencil design. The upper wing has been omitted and the birds are facing right

and left alternately. To get in close to the ceiling like this, the easiest way is to cut a stencil featuring just the two birds, one reversed.

Continue the blue bird theme throughout the room, adding matching decorations to old furniture that has been renovated and painted at very little cost. Even the Lloyd Loom chair sports a bird and bow stencil but in a bolder design to suit the woven texture of the chair. Other ideas for a room like this are stencilled bedlinen or curtain fabric, a bedside mat, or you could even stencil the floorboards if you're feeling really industrious.

Make this simple bedhead decoration using stencils and lots of inexpensive buttermuslin. Start by painting the walls in white emulsion. When dry, mix up a pale blue wash from very diluted sky blue emulsion paint. Use a large brush and swish on lightly over the white to give a soft, slightly streaky finish. If some areas are too strong, soften with a damp cloth whilst still wet.

Find the centre point about, 150cm (5ft) above the bed. Drill and plug a hole and screw in a small brass hook. Find the centre of a 16m (18yd) length of buttermuslin. Gather it up across the width and tie a bow of peach satin ribbon to hold it in place. Tie another bow on to the hook and around the muslin so that you have a double bow. Trim the ribbon ends at various lengths.

Mark either side of the bed about 30cm (12in) below the centre hook. Drape the muslin to find the best shape and insert two brass hooks at the appropriate points. On the buttermuslin, mark equal distances either side of the centre with tape. As before, tie two bows around the muslin just above the tape, and attach to the hook. Remove the tape and hem the drapes.

Draw and cut out stencils of individual birds from the design on page 47. Tape these on to the wall around the hooks holding up the muslin. Stencil with quick-drying stencil paints and a small stencil brush. Mix up a soft blue-grey to tone with the background. Clean the stencils in water straight after use as the tiny holes in this design can easily fill up and get blocked.

A painted Lloyd Loom chair is an ideal accessory for this child's bedroom. As the wall stencil is too detailed for the texture of the chair, a bolder version of the design has been chosen. Use the pattern on page 88 to cut three stencils from acetate. Tape the bow stencil centrally on the chair back and mask all around. Spray with household spray paint in soft peach.

Position a bird stencil on the left of the chair beside the bow. Tape in place and mask as before. Spray the bird in white. Spray several thin coats from about 30cm (12in) away, until the weave of the chair is well covered but not clogged. Leave to dry, then carefully remove the stencil and mask. Repeat with the other bird stencil to complete the design.

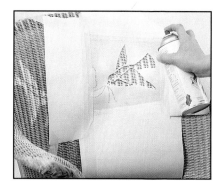

You will need to adapt the original bluebird pattern for this prettily decorated chest of drawers. Trace off the central bow from page 47 and turn the design slightly so that the ribbon tails hang vertically. To balance the bow, sketch in another loop of ribbon on the left. Also use the bow design on page 49.

Trace off the new bow design on to a small piece of acetate using a fine waterproof felt-tipped pen. Mark the position of the bird stencils on either side to align the design when stencilling. Cut out the shapes carefully using a sharp craft knife and a cutting mat. Also make a bird stencil. Alternatively, use part of the complete stencil if you have one already made.

If you are only using part of a complete design, mask off the areas of stencil you do not want with paper and masking tape. Mark the centre of the drawer with a pencil line and stencil either side, reversing the stencil as needed. Use quick-drying stencil paint over a base coat of emulsion and, once dry, finish off with a coat of clear varnish.

Follow the pattern opposite to make your full-size stencil. Trace off the bluebirds on to a sheet of clear acetate using a fine waterproof felt-tipped pen. Also trace off some parts of the peach bows, using a dotted line, to help position the stencil. Mark the top and side lines as register marks, then cut out the bird shapes using a craft knife.

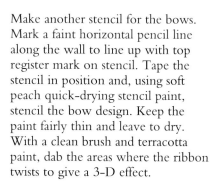

Make another stencil for the bows. Mark a faint horizontal pencil line along the wall to line up with top register mark on stencil. Tape the stencil in position and, using soft peach quick-drying stencil paint, stencil the bow design. Keep the paint fairly thin and leave to dry. With a clean brush and terracotta paint, dab the areas where the ribbon twists to give a 3-D effect.

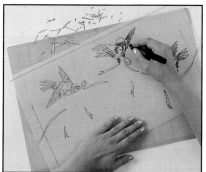

Using the bluebird stencil, tape the acetate in position, lining up your register marks and matching the dotted lines with the stencilled bows. Carefully dab slate blue stencil paint over the birds. Make sure the whole design is covered but keep the brush fairly dry to avoid paint seeping underneath. Wipe the surface often to prevent small holes in the stencil becoming clogged.

One square represents 2cm (¾in)

47

U se this delicate bow to 'hang' small pictures in your bluebird bedroom. The ribbons at the side interlock so you can also use it as a pretty border pattern. Trace off and cut out the design opposite on acetate. Tape the stencil just above the picture so that the ends of the ribbons will disappear behind the frame. Stencil with quick-drying stencil paint in soft peach.

When the paint has dried slightly, use a clean brush to lightly dab on some terracotta colour stencil paint. Do this where the ribbons twist and overlap to give a 3-D effect and make the ribbon look almost shiny. Blend the terracotta paint into the soft peach to avoid a sudden colour change.

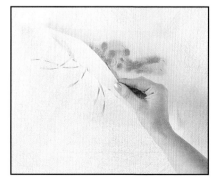

One square represents 1cm (½in)

COUNTRY KITCHEN

T he pretty Dutch-style border tiles were the inspiration for the
fresh floral stencils that enliven an otherwise rather stark kitchen.
The simple kitchen units have a sprayed-on design featuring the tulip-
shaped flower heads arranged formally in an urn. The design is
deliberately symmetrical so that it is adaptable for different widths of
door unit and does not catch and hold the eye too much all over the
room. Even the fridge and dishwasher have been stencilled to match.

If your kitchen cupboards have plain wooden doors, this pattern is
also suitable, provided you use paler or darker shades to the wood to

make the design stand out. Rub varnished surface lightly with steel wool, then use car sprays or quick-drying stencil paints. The flower border is very stylized and is a pattern that can be used successfully either around windows and door frames or singly on a shelf unit. It can even be used over pictures to act as a decorative hanger. It is also an easy design to curve around the table edge or to position in a circular central motif as shown on the table top and chair seats on pages 56-57. You can use a design like this to make the co-ordinated kitchen you've always dreamed of.

S tart by enlarging and cutting out the whole stencil for the door
units (see page 59). You will notice that the left hand door unit in
the picture below is considerably narrower than the one on the right.
The stencil design will fit comfortably in the narrower space, without
looking squashed, if you omit stencilling the outer two petals of the
most extreme left and right blooms, thus turning them into buds. To
do this, lay strips of masking tape over the appropriate areas to block
them out completely. Carefully trim any excess tape covering the
adjoining areas, using a sharp craft knife. You can peel the masking
tape off easily when you have stencilled the narrow door.

C lean the doors thoroughly to remove dirt and all traces of grease before stencilling. Mark the centre lines horizontally and vertically on the acetate. Mark these lines again near the outer edge of each door, using a chinagraph pencil and a set-square and ruler.

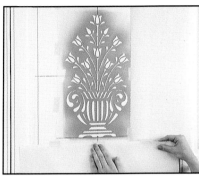

Very lightly cover the back of the stencil sheet with spray glue. This will make it adhere to the vertical surfaces and prevent the spray paint from creeping underneath. Tape the stencil in place, lining up the register marks accurately. Tape sheets of waste paper around the edge of the design to protect the area from overspray.

Use cellulose car spray paints to colour the stencil, spraying gently back and forth from about 30cm (12in) away. Shake the can well before spraying and aim for a light even coating so that the paint does not run. Return after a few moments and add short bursts of spray in certain areas, such as the base of each flower, to enliven the design but don't fill in the stencil too much.

Leave to dry for a few moments and then remove the paper mask to use again. Gently lift off the stencil, checking that the paint has not run underneath. If it has, quickly take a small rag or cotton bud dipped in paint thinners and very carefully wipe away the mistake. Leave stencil overnight to dry hard then clean off the register marks with liquid detergent.

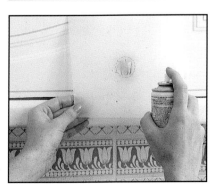

To stencil the handles, cut a small flower in the centre of a 30cm (12in) square sheet of acetate. Spray the back with glue and press in place on handle. Give two light bursts of colour and carefully remove the stencil. Leave to dry hard. These stencils will withstand ordinary washing with detergents but not abrasives. It is possible to remove them with thinners.

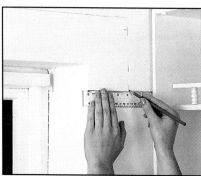

Trace and cut out the tulip border stencil opposite, drawing in lines top and bottom to keep it level. Try it around the window and then mark the wall with a chinagraph pencil to position the design accurately each time. Mark the centre point along the top of the window, where the design will change direction.

Work out how the design will link best at the corner, perhaps using a trial stencil on scrap paper. Start stencilling at the corner and work down towards the sill. Use quick-drying stencil paint in a blue-grey and stencil quite lightly to give a soft, grainy texture. Wipe the acetate occasionally to prevent clogging.

Once again, start at the corner and work across the top of the window. Use masking tape where the design overlaps so that you block out the area already stencilled. Work towards the centre point and stop just before it. Clean the stencil, turn it over and stencil the other half of the window. Lastly, put a single flower head at the centre point to complete.

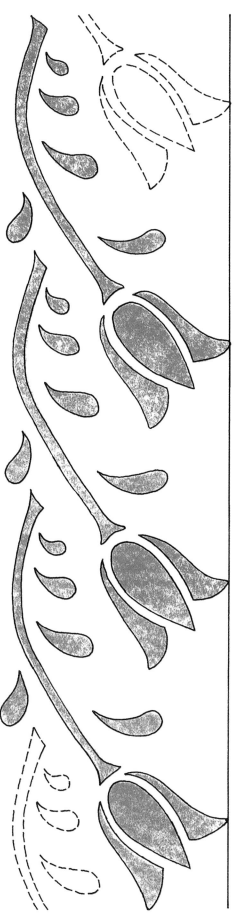

These table and chairs have been ragged in soft blue eggshell paints to go with the kitchen and then stencilled with the tulip design. To decorate the table, find the centre of the table and accurately draw four intersecting pencil lines. Trace off one tulip motif from page 55 and cut out in acetate with a sharp craft knife.

Mark intersecting registration lines on the stencil, making one of the lines run through the centre of the flower. Tape the acetate on to the table, lining up the registration and pencil marks carefully. Stencil with a large brush in white eggshell paint. Apply two light coats before removing the stencil, allowing the paint to become touch-dry between coats to avoid smudging.

Draw the curve of the table edge on to a large sheet of tracing paper. Use the border stencil design to draw out a curved version to fit your table exactly. Simply move the pattern to line up each motif with the curved line and then trace it off. You will need about three motifs. Cut out the stencil and then paint as for the table centre.

The chairs have drop-in seats so it is easy to stencil fabric and staple it in place. Use heavy, white cotton fabric cut 10cm (4in) larger than the seat. Stencil as for the table centre using pale blue fabric paint. Fix with a hot iron when dry. Pull the fabric taut over the seat and staple the corners to the underside first, then staple the sides, working from the middle outwards.

Stencil a pretty pine lampshade to hang over the corner table and complete the setting. Sand the wood smooth and paint with two or three coats of pale blue satin varnish. Use a single flower motif and trim the acetate to fit one section. Place the stencil centrally and draw in the outline of the section to align the stencil accurately each time.

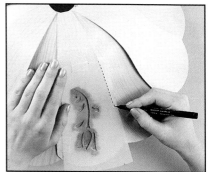

Tape the stencil on one section and stencil all over with quick-drying stencil paint in pale blue. Use a clean brush and lightly shade the base of the flower and leaves with a darker blue-grey paint. Leave to dry and give the whole shade a coat of clear matt varnish to complete it.

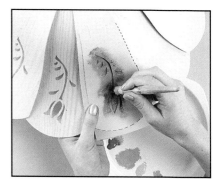

Size as required:
suggest one square
represents 2cm (¾in)

T his hall started out as a rather
bleak modern passageway
but with the clever use of colour
and stencilling it has become a
delightful entrance to welcome
you into the rest of the house.

The border design was drawn
from Italian decorative stone
carvings from the 16th century
and the 'wallpaper' design is
adapted from a Florentine
Renaissance motif. Try out the
border design in a single colour as
well as the two-colour version
used here – it's interesting how
different it can look and, if you
prefer it, you will then only need
to cut one stencil.

The beauty of stencilling
'wallpaper' is that you can
position the motifs exactly where
you want them – no half patterns
as you reach a corner – you just
move the pattern along slightly
and it all fits in. Similarly, uneven
walls and un-square corners can
also be conquered.

The semi-circular table is
stencilled to match the wall
border after being given a
marbled paint finish in grey, beige
and white. The wall border
pattern has been curved to fit the
table and also to go around the
top of the mirror which helps to
lighten and enlarge the area.
There are full instructions on
page 65 on how to adapt a
straight border to fit around any
curve so that you can stencil
wherever you choose.

Trace off the Florentine motif from page 92. Draw out the pattern carefully, spacing the motifs evenly about 9cm (3½in) apart vertically and 7.5cm (3in) apart horizontally. You will need two motifs minimum for small areas but you will greatly speed up the stencilling if you cut a sheet with six or eight motifs. Also draw on vertical guidelines and dotted motif outlines.

Find the centre of the wall and use a plumb-line to mark a vertical pencil line down to the dado rail. Join up the pencil marks with a long ruler and use this line to begin stencilling.

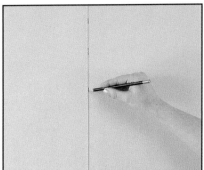

Start near the top of the wall and work one row of motifs vertically down the plumb-line. Make pencil marks first so that the design starts about 5cm (2in) from the ceiling and leaves a 11.5cm (4½in) space above the dado rail for the border. Mix up some grey quick-drying stencil paint and brush stencil lightly to give a soft, grainy texture.

When using a small, two-motif stencil, overlap the lower motif you have stencilled with the top one on the acetate sheet to space the first row accurately. The small stencil is useful in tight corners and close to door frames to prevent bending the acetate too much.

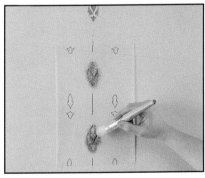

Work the next vertical row of motifs matching up the dotted areas with the first row of stencilling. Continue all over the wall. Adjust the space between rows very slightly to accommodate awkward corners. Stencil within 13cm (5in) of the mirror edge. If there are large gaps near the curved area, leave them and add another motif later when the border is complete.

You will need to curve the stencil border design to fit exactly around a curved table top or mirror. First, trace out your curve on to a large sheet of paper. Size up the border design from page 90, trace it and cut slits alternately into the top and bottom edges of the design so that it will bend easily. Tape the border design in place over your curved line.

Trace the adapted design, extending and curving the lines where needed. Now cut one stencil for each colour. Mark on dotted register lines and also the curved line to follow the table edge, using a waterproof felt-tipped pen. Stencil in white quick-drying stencil paint, dabbing with a large brush to make a soft, grainy texture over the marbling. Leave to dry before removing the stencil.

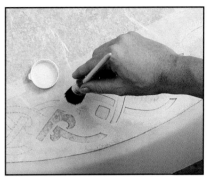

Tape the other stencil sheet in position and stencil with an almost dry brush in blue-grey paint. Dab most of the paint on to kitchen paper before you work on the stencil to achieve a subtle mottled finish that will blend well with the marbling on the table. Varnish to protect when the stencil is dry.

Stencil the straight border on the wall just above the dado rail. Cut the edge of the stencil so that it will run along the dado rail to make measuring unnecessary and stencilling quicker. Use the same stencil paints as for the table top and stencil quite lightly

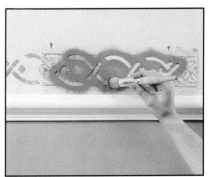

When you reach a corner, at the side of the mirror, lay a piece of masking tape across the stencil at a 45° angle, to mitre the corner. Stencil up to the tape on both stencils. Stencil the curve around the arched top of the mirror first, then work the straight design down towards the dado rail. Mitre the corner again to match up with the rest of the border.

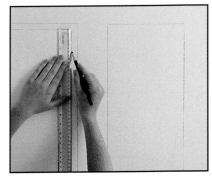

The plain flush doors in this modern hall looked very boring, so to add a little character they have been stencilled with four grey borders to give a panelled look. Start by marking out the panels with pencil lines, using a long ruler and set-square for accuracy. The borders should be about 1.5cm (⁵/₈in) wide, with the space at the bottom of the door greater than the top and sides.

Use long strips of masking tape to mask off around the border, on both sides. Press down the tape with your fingertip to prevent paint from seeping underneath and cut the corners neatly with a sharp craft knife. On an old plate, mix up some white, grey and black quick-drying stencil paints. If the door paint is very shiny, lightly sand the border area first to key the stencilling.

If your light source is on the right, start by stencilling the left hand side of each panel in a medium grey, dabbing the paint on thinly and evenly. Mask the top and bottom corners of this line with tape to form a 45° angle (like the mitred corner of a frame). (If the light comes from the left hand side, start stencilling on the right hand side of each panel.)

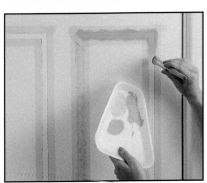

Leave to dry for a few minutes and remove the angled corner tapes. Then stencil the top and right hand border in dark grey. (Top and left hand border, if light comes from the left.) Mask the corners at an angle, as before. Stencil a thin, even coating of colour, getting slightly paler towards the bottom of the panel.

Lastly, stencil the lower border in pale grey as it will theoretically get the most amount of light. Leave to dry and very carefully pull off the masking tape. For economy, these tapes can be used several times. Stencil all the other panels on the door and then clean off the pencil marks with a damp cloth when the paint has dried.

-HONEYSUCKLE BATHROOM -

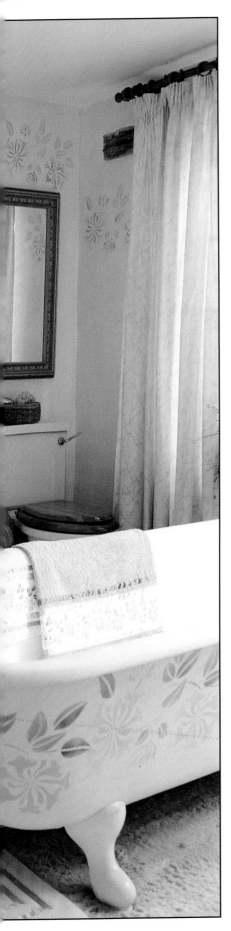

Bring a touch of sophistication to a simple bathroom with this flamboyant honeysuckle stencil. Even the traditional roll-top bath can be restored and decorated to make it a stunning feature standing in the centre of the room. You can use inexpensive household spray paints for this, stencilling after you have coated the outside with a smooth protective spray finish. The design works equally well as a tiny border stencilled on fabric to decorate plain towels or enlarged and sponge stencilled on to roughly sponged yellow walls. Use it as a single motif or join several to make a flowing border pattern. Bathrooms can so often be rather 'cold' with the traditional use of pastel colours. Stencilling provides the ideal opportunity to develop a whole new approach to decorating your bathroom.

Enlarge and cut out two stencils from the honeysuckle design opposite. Clean the outside of the bath thoroughly – you can spray paint this first if necessary. Spray glue over the back of the first stencil and tape in place. Mask all around with plenty of waste paper to protect from overspray. Using household spray paint, held about 30cm (12in) away, spray the flowers lightly in yellow.

Leave to dry for a few moments. Meanwhile, shake a can of pink spray paint to mix it thoroughly. When the first colour is touch-dry, spray the centre of each circle of flowers with a burst of pink to subtly shade it.

Tape the leaf stencil in place, lining up the flowers with the dotted lines on the acetate. Tape waste paper all around as before and lightly spray the leaves in green. Add a little extra green in a few places to liven it up. Stencil all around the bath, then leave the paint to dry thoroughly before use.

T race the yellow part of the
honeysuckle design straight
from page 71 on to clear acetate
using a fine waterproof felt-tipped
pen. Draw in the upper and lower
registration lines and also a few
leaves to help position the stencil
accurately. Using a craft knife and
cutting mat, cut out the yellow parts
of the design. Make a separate stencil
for the green leaves.

Pin or tape a piece of old fabric on to your work surface. Tape a strip of white poplin on to this and draw registration lines in faint pencil to match those on the stencil. Lay the green stencil on top and apply a mixture of green and yellow fabric paints with a dry brush.

Complete the green border, then stencil the yellow flowers and buds. Start with yellow around the outer parts of the flowers, then blend pink in the centre. Leave the fabric paint to dry, then fix it following the manufacturer's instructions. Cut out the stencilled fabric along the pencil lines to fit the width of the towel.

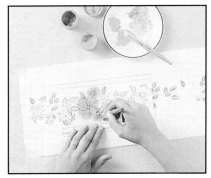

Sew the stencilled strip along the long raw edges on to the towel; turn under the short raw edges to neaten. Pin a length of green satin ribbon over both raw edges and stitch down both sides of the ribbon. Sew on two more pieces of narrower peach ribbon either side.

To make a stencil for the bath mat, you must enlarge the design on page 71. You can do this by following the squares on the printed pattern and drawing the design square by square on to a larger grid. The squares of your grid should measure 5cm (2in) each.

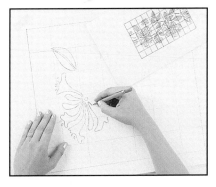

Use fabric paints to stencil one large honeysuckle motif on to the centre panel of a plain peach bath mat. First press the mat and tape it to your work surface. Tape the stencil in place and dab fabric paint on to the towelling. You will need quite a lot of paint since the fabric is textured and absorbent. Fix the paint when dry and add ribbons to match the towels.

To create this beautiful effect, first paint your walls in white silk vinyl and then sponge pale, sunny yellow emulsion paint over the top to make a warm, cloudy effect. Dip a large, damp natural sponge into a saucer of paint, taking care not to overload the sponge. Dab off the excess on to a spare piece of cardboard, then dab on to the wall in an even pattern.

Enlarge and cut two stencil sheets from the design on page 71. Lightly mark the desired level on the wall and tape the flower stencil in place. Use a small piece of natural sponge and dip it into a saucer containing pale peach or yellow stencil paint or emulsion paint. Tester pots are ideal for this purpose. Dab on to the stencil around the edge of each circle of flowers.

Mix up a subtle pinky-orange and sponge-stencil this on to the centre of each group of flowers. Gradually blend the pink with the yellow to make a soft orange. Stencil all the flowers around the wall like this, linking the design with the dotted lines on the stencil.

Tape on the leaf stencil and mix a few shades of green from lime to emerald on an old plate. Use another piece of sponge to stencil the leaves and stems. Try to vary the shades of green over the design, to give added interest. Dab lightly for a mottled texture that blends with the wall sponging.

Choose two or three warm colours and subtle textures for a rich, elegant mood in a small study. Don't worry that it will make the room seem smaller – privacy is important! Keep the stencilling classically simple to stop it becoming too distracting. Pictures are important and these are accentuated by a two-colour rope border that can be stencilled around a group of prints to make an attractive 'frame'. The loop and tassels add interesting detail – double tassels for large pictures and single ones under smaller prints. Below the dado rail is the boldest colour with a paler version ragged on top, giving an almost leather-like quality.

The accessories are simple but become part of the whole theme with touches of the rope border in either the same shades or with gold and copper lustre to add sparkle.

The chintz tablecloth and re-vamped wooden tablelamp and shade look rich and expensive in the matching colours but imagine the same items stencilled in shades of pink and peach on cream and white with a touch of silver. A transformation, making them look pretty and delicate to fit perfectly into an alcove in a guest bedroom or landing. Have fun experimenting with the designs in a wide range of colours and situations to change the mood and style.

Decorate a simple DIY pine letter rack, then stencil notepaper to match, for a lovely gift or a smart desk accessory. Sand the wood smooth and cut out two stencil sheets from the small curved rope design opposite. Tape the first stencil on to the wood and use quick-drying stencil paints, mixed up to match your decor, to stencil the first half of your design.

Match up the remainder of the design on the second stencil sheet and paint the second colour. Temporarily assemble the four walls of the letter rack with tape and stencil the large rope design (see page 93) around the lower edge of the box in the same colours.

Now glue the box together using PVA wood glue. Begin with the four walls, then, when dry, glue these to the base. The centre section will then just slide into place. Glue this if you wish. Varnish the letter rack with several coats of clear polyurethane varnish to give a smooth, durable finish and to protect the stencilling.

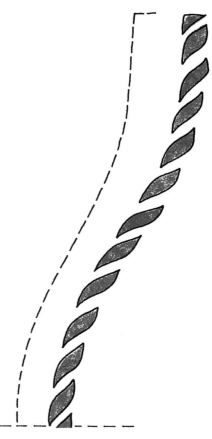

Choose an assortment of notepaper and envelopes in subtle tones to go with your letter rack. Use the same stencils to decorate the top of some sheets, working with oil-based stencil crayons. Rub a little crayon on to a corner of the stencil or a spare piece of acetate and then collect the colour on to a brush. Stencil the colour on to the paper using a circular movement.

Above: Use this pattern to cut out your curved stencils for the top of the letter rack and the notepaper. It only shows half of the design, so trace it off marking on the straight dotted centre line. Then turn the tracing over, match up the design, and trace in the other half accurately.

Decorate envelopes to match using the stencil crayons. Use a simple design along the lower edge or just a single motif that will not get in the way of the written address. Leave the stencilling to set for a while before using the notepaper and envelopes, to avoid smudging.

Draw and cut out the corner and straight rope border design, plus the loop and tassel designs, from pages 92-93; cut two stencils for each. Hang up a group of pictures on your wall. Temporarily tape a loop and a tassel stencil sheet in place and then mark a pencil line for the border. Use a plumb-line, set-square and long ruler for accuracy and leave an even margin around the pictures.

Starting in one lower corner, tape the rope corner stencil in place. Mix up quick-drying stencil paints and stencil lightly, accentuating the colour along the lower edge of each shape to resemble a shadow. Stencil in the second colour, matching up the dotted register lines and the straight, edge lines.

Now, stencil away from the corner, using the straight rope stencil. Move the corner stencil to the far lower corner and stencil up to it, to match the pattern. Move the border very slightly, if necessary, to join the design perfectly. Work all around the panel in both colours and leave the border to dry.

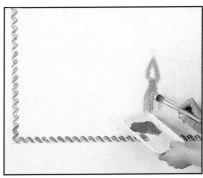

Remove the picture and stencil both the tassel colours to match the border. You can use a single tassel, placed centrally under a small picture, or a double tassel under a large picture. In the latter instance, try out the angles to overlap the tassels on paper first, then work on the wall. Make sure the tassels are placed exactly under the centre of the picture.

Lastly, stencil the top loop over the picture in the same way. Mark the exact position by running a pencil horizontally along the top of the picture frame and then marking a vertical plumb-line down to the centre of the tassel. The ends of the loop should disappear behind the picture frame to complete the rope hanging illusion.

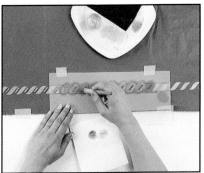

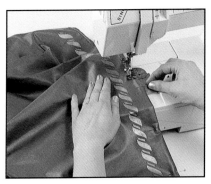

Make a round, full-length table-cloth and a square top cloth for a circular or hexagonal table. Measure twice the width of the table for the square cloth and cut out in green chintz. Tape the straight rope border stencil near the edge of the fabric. Dip the brush into gold lustre fabric paint, wipe off excess and then dip into gold 'bronzing' powder tipped on to a piece of velvet.

Stencil all around, using the corner stencils as necessary (see page 93). Tape on the other stencil in the set and use silver lustre fabric paint and silver 'bronzing' powder to finish the rope design. Use the velvet to dispense the silver powder on to the brush sparingly and evenly. Stencil a tassel in each corner too. Leave to dry for several days then set with a hot iron.

Turn under a narrow hem all around the raw edge of the cloth and press, then pin in place. Set the sewing machine on to a very close spaced zig-zag stitch to look like satin stitch. Sew all around in contrasting thread to make a decorative border that neatens the raw edge.

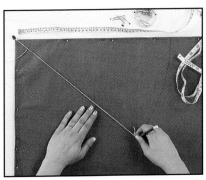

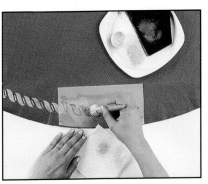

To work out the radius of your round cloth, measure from the centre of the table down to the floor. Join widths of chintz to make a square of fabric measuring twice the radius. Fold the fabric into four and pin. Insert a drawing-pin into the corner that is the centre of the fabric. Attach some string tied to a pencil, making the distance from the pin equal to the radius. Now draw an arc.

Cut out the cloth 1.5cm (⅝in) outside the arc, through all four layers to make a circle. Unpin, open out and press. Using a curved version of the rope design, as for the lampshade, stencil the edge of the cloth in the same way as the square one. Turn under the raw edge and work satin-stitch using matching colour thread.

This old, turned wooden lamp base was repainted to give it a new lease of life. Sand the lamp base and spray with several coats of green paint. Leave until touch-dry between coats, and for at least a day once finished, to dry hard. Then press strips of masking tape around the lamp base to leave several narrow bands exposed.

Wrap tissue paper around the lamp base, taping it in place to protect it from the gold spray. Shake a can of gold household paint thoroughly to mix and then spray several light coats to colour the exposed areas. Carefully remove the tissue paper and pull off the tape, then leave each stripe to dry thoroughly. Add as many stripes and borders as you like.

The gold-edged lampshade has been decorated with a rope design border from page 93. Use the same method as for the hall table on page 65 to curve the design to fit. Cut one stencil. Tape it on to the shade and then draw on the curved lampshade edge to align the pattern correctly each time.

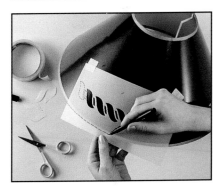

Cover the whole lampshade with tissue paper to protect it from overspray, just leaving the stencil exposed. Tape the paper in place, all around, on to the acetate and then stencil using gold household spray. Work about 30cm (12in) away from the shade and apply several light coats. If necessary, spray glue on to the back of the stencil to hold it pressed flat against the shade.

Work around the shade, carefully peeling off the acetate as soon as you have finished stencilling. Leave for a few moments to become touch-dry and place the stencil further along, matching the pattern carefully. Slightly adjust the spacing, if necessary, to match up the design where the beginning and end meet.

TEMPLATES

Square up the stencil designs to the required size as described on page 10.

Page 16

Suggested size: One
square represents 1.5cm (⁵⁄₈in)

Pages 24-25

Page 16

Pages 18-19

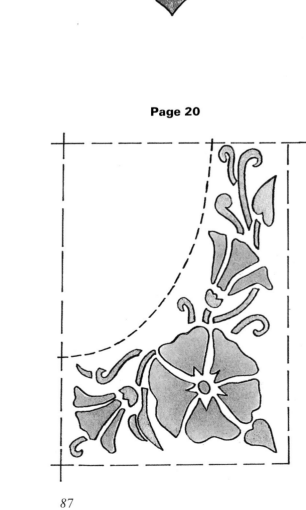

Page 20

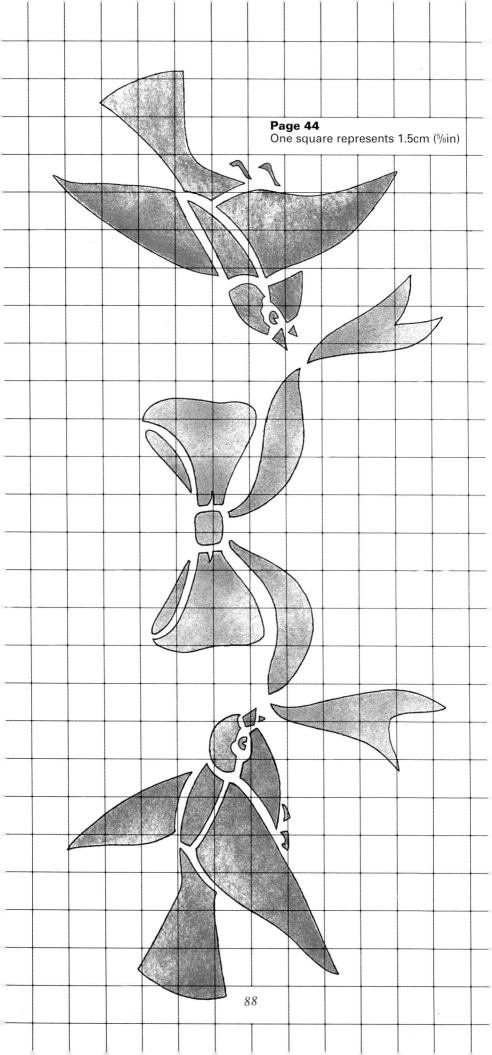

Page 44
One square represents 1.5cm (⁵/₈in)

Pages 32-35
One square represents 1.5cm ($^5/_8$in)

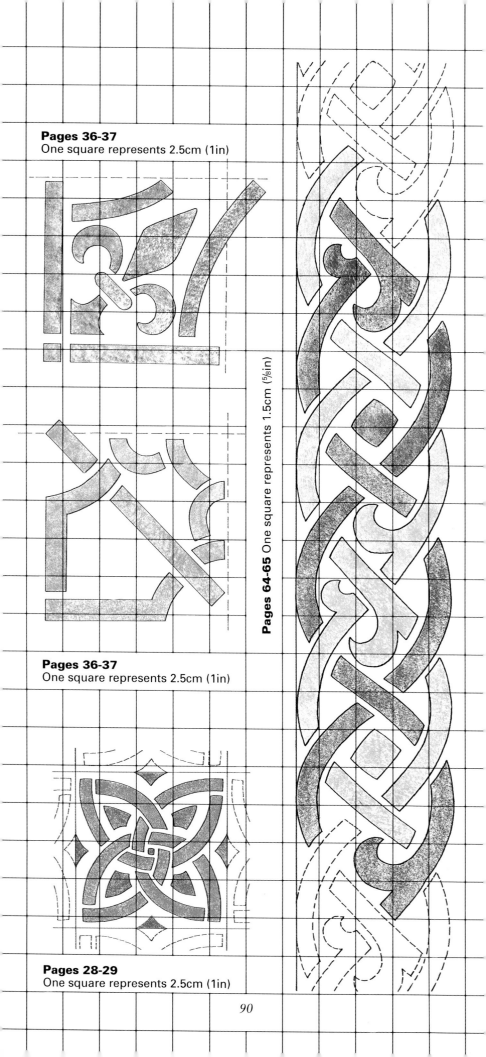

Pages 36-37
One square represents 2.5cm (1in)

Pages 36-37
One square represents 2.5cm (1in)

Pages 64-65 One square represents 1.5cm (⅝in)

Pages 28-29
One square represents 2.5cm (1in)

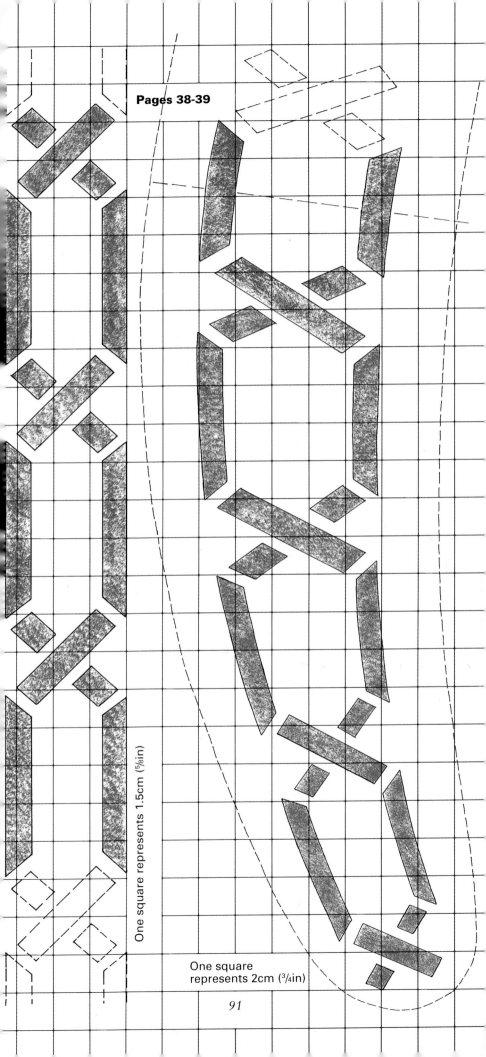

One square represents 1.5cm (⅝in)

One square
represents 2cm (¾in)

Pages 14-15 and 63

Pages 14-15 and 80-81

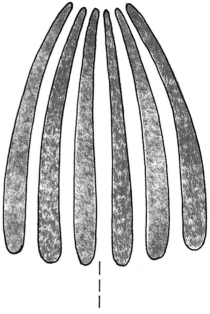

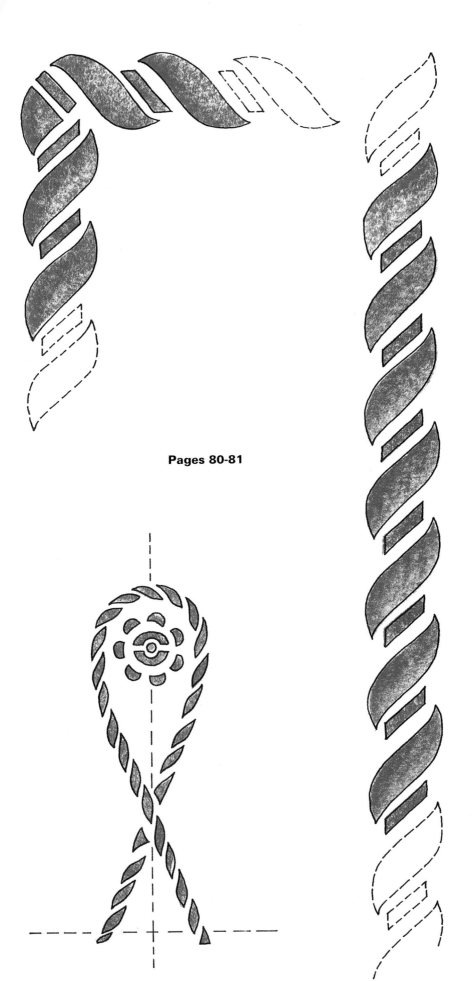

Pages 80-81

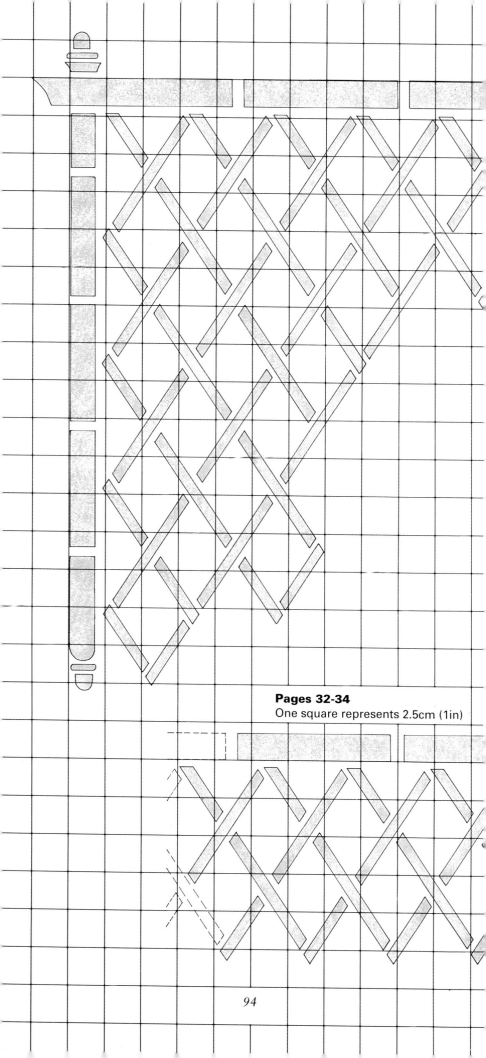

Pages 32-34
One square represents 2.5cm (1in)

94

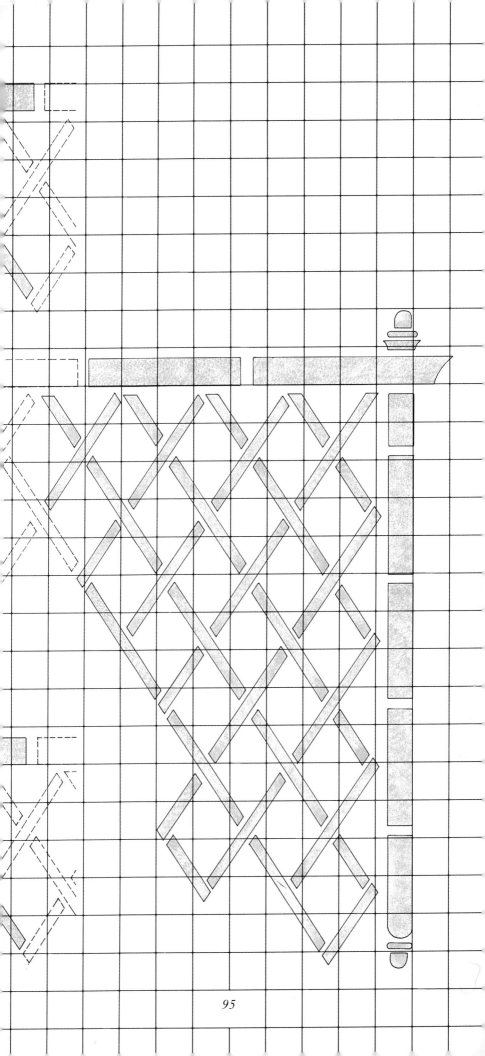

INDEX

ACKNOWLEDGEMENTS

The author and publishers would like to thank the following for their help in compiling this book:

Carolyn Warrender Stencil Designs Ltd. for supplying stencil paints, stencil brushes, Mylar®, bronzing powder and fabric paints
Mail Order: Unit 3, Maple Cross Industrial Estate, Rickmansworth, Hertfordshire WD3 2RA

Crown Paints for supplying all silk and matt emulsion paints used
P.O. Box 37, Crown House, Hollins Road, Darwen, Lancashire BB3 0BG

Panduro Hobby Ltd., mail order suppliers of craft and hobby products
Westway House, Transport Avenue, Brentford, Middlesex TW8 9HF

Eurostudio for supplying stencil acetate, crayons and brushes
Unit 4, Southdown Industrial Estate, Southdown Road, Harpenden, Hertfordshire

Ian Mankin Ltd., specialist suppliers of all natural fabrics, for supplying calico
109 Regents Park Road, London NW1 8UR

English Abrasives Ltd. for supplying household spray paints
P.O. Box 85, Marsh Lane, London N17 0XA

Anne and Vince of V & A Traynor Fine Arts for lending pictures and supplying picture mounts
5 Oakmede Place, Binfield, Berkshire RG12 5JF

Tootal Craft Ltd., for supplying ribbons and lace
Units 1 and 2, Westpoint Enterprise Park, Clarence Avenue, Trafford Park, Manchester M17 1QS

Special thanks also go to Kirsty and Kevin for lending their cottage and preparing the rooms for stencilling.